An unseen smile is more reassuring than a pseudo-crowd bubbling with laughter.

- **F.Omosola**

All rights reserved. No part of this publication may be reproduced, distributed, or transmitted in any form or by any means, including photocopying, recording, or other electronic or mechanical methods, without the prior written permission of the publisher, except in the case of brief quotations embodied in critical reviews and certain other non-commercial uses permitted by copyright law.

FORTUNE OMOSOLA © 2023

ISBN (Paperback) - 978-1-917267-20-5

ISBN (E-Book) - 978-1-917267-21-2

Published by Nubian Republic on behalf of Palmwine Publishing Limited Nigeria

Email: info@palmwinepublishing.com

Address- UK: 86-90, Paul Street, London EC2A 4NE

Address-Nigeria: 1A Jos Road Bukuru, Plateau State, Nigeria.

www.palmwinepublishing.com
www.raffiapress.com
www.nuciferaanalysis.com

Acknowledgements

My sincere appreciation to establish authors of poetry publications and other creative I from n Nigeria and outside, whose undiluted knowledge of expanse I have tapped from.

Regards to my wife, Brie, my kids, Queen and Empress who allowed me time away from Daddy duties to write this budding interest of mine.

Special thanks as well to my more and friends who had no idea this was under wraps I am sure would be surprised at this special publication.

Most importantly, I bring to my mind those who would come in contact with this book, I hope it will resonate with you and keep you yearning for something more.

Table of Contents

Acknowledgements   3

Foreword   6

CHAPTER 1
Introduction to Poetry   8

CHAPTER 2
Forms of Poetry   11

CHAPTER 3
Imagery and Figurative Language   17

CHAPTER 4
Themes in Poetry   26

CHAPTER 5
Sound and Rhythm   36

CHAPTER 6
Poetic Devices   40

CHAPTER 7
The Poet's Voice and Style   46

CHAPTER 8
Interpreting Poetry   51

CHAPTER 9
Writing   56

CHAPTER 10
The future of Poetry   61

References   67
About the Author

FOREWORD

Poetry is an art form that has captivated the hearts and minds of people for centuries. It is a medium of expression that allows us to convey our deepest emotions, thoughts and ideas in a way that transcends language. The power of poetry lies in its ability to evoke emotions, stir imaginations, and transport readers to another world.

In "The Nuances of Poetry," the author has done a remarkable job of exploring the different facets of poetry and providing readers with a comprehensive understanding of this art form. This book is a valuable resource for anyone who wishes to deepen their appreciation and understanding of poetry, from students and scholars to poetry enthusiasts and casual readers.

This chapbook is divided into ten chapters that cover various aspects of poetry, including the different forms of poetry, themes, imagery, figurative language, sound and rhythm, poetic devices, and the poet's voice and style. The author has also included examples of poems from notable Nigerian, African, and Western poets to illustrate their points and provide context.

One of the standout features of this book is its focus on African poetry. The author highlights the contributions of African poets to the world of poetry and shows how their unique perspectives and experiences have shaped their work. This emphasis on African poetry is particularly significant given the rich poetic traditions that exist on the continent.

In addition to its focus on African poetry, the book also includes examples from Western poets such as Shakespeare, Dickinson, Frost, Plath, and Eliot. This diversity of voices and perspectives helps to illustrate the universality of poetry and its ability to transcend cultural and geographical boundaries.

As a reader and poetry lover, you will find this book to be engaging, informative, and thought-provoking. It is a testament to the beauty and complexity of poetry and the role it plays in our lives. Whether you are a seasoned poetry enthusiast or a newcomer to the world of poetry, "The Nuances of Poetry" is a must-read.

Bukola F.Omosola

(Broadcaster, Creative)

CHAPTER 1

Introduction to Poetry

Poetry is a unique and complex art form that has been around for centuries. It is a form of creative writing that uses language in a way that transcends ordinary communication, using words to create a sensory experience that evokes emotions and thoughts.

At its core, poetry is about communication. It is a way for the poet to express their ideas and emotions, and for the reader to experience those ideas and emotions. Poetry uses language in a way that is different from other forms of writing, using sound, rhythm, and imagery to convey meaning.

One of the defining features of poetry is its use of figurative language. Poets use metaphors, similes, personification, and other literary devices to create comparisons and associations that convey meaning and emotion. For example, in the poem "Hope" by Emily Dickinson, she uses the metaphor of a bird to represent hope, saying:

"Hope is the thing with feathers / That perches in the soul."

This metaphor creates a vivid image that helps the reader understand the abstract concept of hope.

Another important aspect of poetry is its use of form. Poets use various forms of poetry, including sonnets, haikus, and free verse, to create structure and rhythm. Each form has its own unique rules and constraints, which the poet can use to create meaning and effect.

Poetry also has the power to evoke emotions and create a sensory experience for the reader. Poets use imagery to create vivid and detailed descriptions that engage the reader's senses.

For example, in the poem "I Wandered Lonely as a Cloud" by William Wordsworth, he describes the beauty of a field of daffodils, saying:

"Continuous as the stars that shine / And twinkle on the Milky Way, / They stretched in never-ending line / Along the margin of a bay."

This description creates a visual image that transports the reader to the scene.

In this book, we will explore the different elements of poetry and how they work together to create meaning and effect. We will examine the different forms of poetry, the use of figurative language, imagery, sound, and rhythm, as well as the poet's voice and style.

We will also explore the unique perspective of African poetry and the contributions of African poets to the world of poetry. African poetry is rich in history, culture, and tradition, and has played a significant role in shaping the literary landscape of the continent.

Throughout this book, we will use examples of poems from notable Nigerian, African, and Western poets to illustrate our points and provide context. By the end of this book, we hope that you will have a deeper appreciation and understanding of the nuances of poetry, and how this art form has the power to enrich our lives and connect us to each other.

CHAPTER 2

Forms of Poetry

One of the distinguishing features of poetry is its use of form. Forms of poetry refer to the structure or organization of a poem, including the length of lines, number of stanzas, rhyme scheme, and meter. There are many different forms of poetry, each with its own unique set of rules and conventions. Understanding the various forms of poetry is essential for analyzing and appreciating poetry.

Sonnets are a popular form of poetry that originated in Italy. A sonnet consists of 14 lines and follows a specific rhyme scheme. The most common rhyme scheme for a sonnet is **ABAB CDCD EFEF GG,** where the letters represent the end rhymes of the lines. The sonnet typically follows a specific pattern of iambic pentameter, which refers to a rhythmic pattern of 10 syllables per line. Examples of sonnets include "Sonnet 18" by William Shakespeare, "How Do I Love Thee" by Elizabeth Barrett Browning, and "On His Blindness" by John Milton.

Haiku is another popular form of poetry that originated in Japan. A haiku consists of three lines and follows a 5-7-5 syllable pattern. Haiku typically focuses on nature and uses imagery to create a sensory experience for the reader. An example of a haiku is "An old silent pond / A frog jumps into the pond— / Splash! Silence again." by Matsuo Basho.

Free verse is a form of poetry that does not follow a specific rhyme scheme or meter. Free verse allows poets to break traditional rules and conventions and create their own structure. Free verse is often used to express personal experiences and emotions. Examples of free verse include "The Waste Land" by T.S. Eliot, "Song of Myself" by Walt Whitman, and "Poem for Maya" by Nikki Giovanni.

Other forms of poetry include the ballad, the ode, the epic, and the elegy, each with its unique characteristics and conventions. It is important to note that some poets may use multiple forms in a single poem or create their own hybrid form.

Understanding the various forms of poetry is important for analyzing and appreciating poetry. Form can affect the meaning. The form effect of a poem and the use of form can be a deliberate choice by the poet. For example, a sonnet may be used to express love or desire, while a haiku may be used to express a moment of stillness or reflection.

In African poetry, there are also various forms. For example, the griot tradition in West Africa uses oral poetry to tell stories and preserve history. The Ewe people of Ghana have a form of poetry called Atsiagbekɔ, which is used in traditional dances and celebrations.

In this chapter, we have explored some of the various forms of poetry and how they are used to create structure and effect. By understanding the different forms of poetry, readers can gain a deeper appreciation for the art form and its complexities.

Here are some excerpts and examples of the different forms of poetry discussed in Chapter 2:

Sonnets:

"Shall I compare thee to a summer's day? / Thou art more lovely and more temperate" - Sonnet 18 by William Shakespeare

"How do I love thee? Let me count the ways. / I love thee to the depth and breadth and height / My soul can reach" - Sonnet 43 by Elizabeth Barrett Browning

"When I consider how my light is spent / Ere half my days in this dark world and wide" - "On His Blindness" by John Milton

Haiku:

"An old silent pond / A frog jumps into the pond— / Splash! Silence again." - Matsuo Basho

"The light of a candle / Is transferred to another candle— / Spring twilight" - Yosa Buson

"The winter moon, / I can't describe the snow / From last month / Remain in the bowl." - Matsuo Basho

---

Free verse:

"April is the cruellest month, breeding cruelest out of the dead land, mixing / Memory and desire, stirring / Dull roots with spring rain." - "The Waste Land" by T.S. Eliot

"I celebrate myself, and sing myself, / And what I assume you shall assume, / For every atom belonging to me as good belongs to you." - "Song of Myself" by Walt Whitman

"We are not lovers / because of the love / we make / but the love / we have" - "Poem for Maya" by Nikki Giovanni

Ballad:

"Oh, Shenandoah, I long to see you / Away, you rolling river / Oh, Shenandoah, I long to see you / Away, I'm bound away / 'Cross tI's

boundissouri" - *radical American ballad*

"Bonny Barbara Allan / When cockle shells turn silver bells / And fishes sing in the sea / And when the moon shines bright at night / Twill be a good time for me" - traditional Scottish ballad

CHAPTER 3

Imagery and Figurative Language

In this chapter, we will explore the importance of imagery and figurative language in poetry. Imagery is the use of language to create sensory impressions and convey meaning beyond the literal level. It includes the use of metaphor, simile, personification, hyperbole, and other figures of speech.

In poetry, imagery refers to the use of words or phrases that create sensory experiences for the reader. It helps the reader to visualize and connect with the emotions and ideas that the poet is trying to convey. There are several types of imagery, which poets use to create meaning in their work:

Visual Imagery - refers to images that can be seen, such as colors, shapes, and objects. For example, "the golden sun sank behind the mountains" creates a visual image of a setting sun.

Auditory Imagery - refers to sounds and noises. For example, "the wind howled through the trees" creates an auditory image of the wind.

Olfactory Imagery - refers to smells and scents. For example, "the aroma of fresh-baked bread filled the air" creates an olfactory image of bread.

Gustatory Imagery - refers to taste. For example, "the sour taste of a lemon made her mouth pucker" creates a gustatory image of a lemon.

Tactile Imagery - refers to touch and texture. For example, "the rough bark of the tree scraped against her skin" creates a tactile image of the tree bark.

In addition to imagery, poets often use figurative language to create meaning in their work.

Examples of poetic language from African poets like Chinua Achebe and Wole Soyinka, as well as Western poets like William Shakespeare and Emily Dickinson.

Poetic Language from African Poets:

"Things Fall Apart" by Chinua Achebe:

"The sun will shine on those who stand before it shines on those who kneel under them."

"Telephone Conversation" by Wole Soyinka:

"The price seemed reasonable, location Indifferent.

The landlady swore she lived Off premises. Nothing remOnethe d But self-confession. 'Madam,' I warned, 'I hate a wasted journey—I am African.'"

"Vultures" by Chinua Achebe:

"In whose hope, except in yours, did this pair of sleek birds / Who ride the warm winds of the heavens, to hawk / For blood, pounce on your household?"

Poetic Language from Western Poets:

"Sonnet 18" by William Shakespeare:

"Shall I compare thee to a summer's day? / Thou art more lovely and more temperate: / Rough winds do shake the darling buds of May, / And summer's lease hath all too short a date."

"Because I Could Not Stop for Death" by Emily Dickinson:

"Because I could not stop for Death / He kindly stopped for me— / The Carriage held but just Ourselves— / And Immortality."

"Ode to a Nightingale" by John Keats:

"Thou wast not born for death, immortal Bird! / No hungry generations tread thee down; / The voice I hear this passing night was heard / In ancient days by emperor and clown."

Let us bring into context some popular poetic languages:

Metaphor is a comparison A metaphor is two unlike thin without ut us, in the words "like" or "as." For example, in Fortune Omosola's poem "Forbidden fruits, a delight to worms," metaphorical language is used to describe the consequences of indulging in forbidden pleasures. The "forbidden fruits" are a metaphor for indulging in things that are harmful to us, and the line "delight to worms" emphasizes the idea that the consequences of indulging in forbidden pleasures can be harmful and self-destructive.

Simile is a comparison between two things that are similar using the words "like" or "as." For example, in Chinua Achebe's poem "Vultures," he uses a simile to describe the namelessness of evil.

> *He writes, "Thus the Commandant at Belsen/ Camp going home for/ the day with fumes of human roast clinging/ rebelliously to his hairy nostrils/ will stop at the wayside sweet-shop/ and pick up a chocolate for his tender offspring/ waiting at home for Daddy's return..."*

Achebe compares the actions of the Commandant to a casual act of picking up chocolate for his children, highlighting the evil nature of his actions.

Personification is the attribution of human qualities to non-human objects or concepts. For example, in William Shakespeare's Sonnet 18, he personifies death as a personified force that is unable to conquer love. He writes, "And Death shall have no dominion." This line implies that love is immortal and cannot be defeated even by death.

Hyperbole is an exaggeration used for emphasis or effect. For example, in Emily Dickinson's poem "Because I could not stop for Death," she uses hyperbole to describe the journey of life.

Analyzing the Nuances of Poetry through the Works of Fortune Omosola

In the world of poetry, a poet's use of language, imagery, and symbolism can convey complex emotions and ideas. Fortune Omosola's poems are an excellent example of this. In this chapter, we will delve into the nuances of poetry by examining the themes and poetic devices used in Omosola's works.

Forbidden fruits, delight to worms,

old pages, bidding the storm,

the charcoal of the orient is burning,

these tales won't make it to moonlight,

but how do you win back apples without a fight?

A man is wary between the sticks, his lamp is the old yellow leaves in winter.

In this poem, Omosola uses metaphorical language to describe the consequences of indulging in forbidden pleasures. The "forbidden fruits" are a metaphor for indulging in things that are harmful to us. The line "delight to worms" emphasizes the idea that the consequences of indulging in forbidden pleasures can be harmful and self-destructive.

The second line, "old pages, bidding the storm," could represent the fleeting nature of time and the impermanence of life. The "charcoal of the orient burning" might signify the destructive power of desire and temptation.

The poem's closing lines, "a man is wary between the sticks, his lamp is the old yellow leaves in winter," portray the struggle of the human spirit to resist temptation. The "sticks" could represent the crossroads of life where one must make decisions. The "lamp" and "old yellow leaves in winter" might symbolize the fleeting nature of life and the need to make the most of one's time.

Let your name honour the king

in honor of cold, warmth

before the gaze of the samurai,

an unquenchable delight

Let the war chariots temper even

as you stand, intrepid.

to place your wrath

the Palace will fall

let your name honour the king

This poem emphasizes the idea of loyalty and honor. The phrase "let your name honor the king" could represent the importance of one's reputation and how it can be an essential part of one's legacy. The "crisp of cold, warmth" and "tepid gaze of the samurai" convey the idea that one should remain steadfast and committed, even in the face of adversity.

The lines "an unquenchable delight" and "Let the war chariots temper even" suggest that a strong will and sense of purpose are necessary to achieve greatness. The final lines, "to place your praline Palace will fall, let your name honor the king," could represent the idea that one's actions can have a significant impact on others and even change the course of history.

The spirit yawns,

enlightened?not yet,

pieces of flesh roam,

untested,

fermented in dimming corals.

This poem seems to explore the concept of enlightenment and spiritual growth. The "spirit yawns" might represent the initial stages of self-discovery, while "enlightened? not yet" suggests that there is still much to learn.

The phrase "pieces of flesh roam, untested" conveys the idea that one's physical body is but a small part of the whole self. The line "fermented in dimming corals" could represent the idea that growth and transformation are sometimes painful but ultimately lead to enlightenment.

CHAPTER 4

Themes in Poetry

Themes in poetry are the underlying ideas, messages, or concepts that are explored and conveyed through the words, images, and symbols used in the poem. A theme is a fundamental and recurring subject that is central to the poem's meaning, and it can be expressed through a wide range of literary devices, such as metaphor, imagery, and symbolism.

Poets often use themes to explore universal human experiences, such as love, death, identity, and social issues, and to express their perspectives. Themes can also be used to explore broader historical, cultural, and political contexts, and to engage with the complexities and contradictions of the world around us.

Themes in poetry can be expressed in a variety of ways, from direct statements or explicit imagery to more subtle or nuanced approaches. They can also be explored through different poetic forms, such as sonnets, haikus, or free verse, and can be influenced by the poet's cultural background, personal experiences, and artistic style. Ultimately, themes in poetry help to create meaning for the reader, allowing them to engage with and interpret the poem in their own unique way.

These can be some examples:

Love and relationships

Nature

Politics and social issues

Identity and self-discovery

Death and mortality

Here are a few examples of how Nigerian and African poets have explored the themes mentioned earlier:

Love and Relationships:

Nigerian poet Chinua Achebe's poem "Marriage is a Private Affair" explores the theme of love and relationships in the context of traditional African values and beliefs. The poem tells the story of a young couple who fall in love despite the objections of their families, and how their lhowiumphs over societal expectations.

One famous poem that also explores the complexities of love is Elizabeth Barrett Browning's

"How Do I Love Thee?" which begins, "How do I love thee? Let me count the ways."

Nature:

African poets have long celebrated the beauty and majesty of the African landscape. South African poet Mongane Wally Serote's poem "To a Wreath of Water-lilies" is a beautiful tribute to the natural beauty of the African continent, while Kenyan poet Ngwatilo Mawiyoo's "There is something in the Water" explores the relationship between humans and the natural world.

Poets have celebrated the beauty and majesty of nature, while also grappling with its destructive forces. William Wordsworth's "I Wandered Lonely as a Cloud" is a classic example of a poem that celebrates the beauty of nature, while Robert Frost's "Stopping by Woods on a Snowy Evening" explores the darker, more ominous aspects of the natural world.

Politics and Social Issues:

African poets have used their work to explore the complex political and social issues facing the continent. Nigerian poet Wole Soyinka's "Telephone Conversation" is a powerful critique of racial discrimination and prejudice, while South African poet Antjie Krog's "The Stars Say 'Tsala' (Go Ahead)" explores the legacy of apartheid and the challenges facing South Africa in the post-apartheid era.

Poets have used their work to critique social inequality, to condemn war and oppression, and to champion civil rights and human dignity. Langston Hughes' poem "Let America Be America Again" is a powerful example of poetry that critiques the American Dream, while Maya Angelou's "Still I Rise" celebrates the resilience and strength of African American women.

Identity and Self-Discovery:

African poets have used their work to explore questions of identity and self-discovery in the context of African culture and history. Nigerian poet Ben Okri's "An African Elegy" is a powerful exploration of the African experience, while Senegalese poet Léopold Sédar Senghor's "Prayer to the Masks" explores the relationship between

African identity and the cultural traditions of the continent.

Poets have used their work to explore their own sense of self, well as to grapple with larger questions of cultural and national identity. Walt Whitman's "Song of Myself" is a classic example of a poem that explores the self in relation to the largeraboutT.S. Eliot's "The Love Song of J. Alfred Prufrock" is a poem that explores the sense of self in relation to others.

Death and mortality

African poets have explored the themes of death and mortality in a variety of ways, from the celebration of life to the contemplation of the afterlife. Nigerian poet Christopher Okigbo's "Elegy for Alto" is a poignant tribute to a friend who died during the Biafran War, while Ghanaian poet Kofi Awoonor's "Songs of Sorrow" is a collection of poems that explores the themes of death and mourning in the context of African culture and tradition.

Emily Dickinson's "Because I could not stop for Death" is a classic example of a poem that explores the theme of mortality, while Dylan Thomas' "Do not go gentle into that good night" is a poem that celebrates the beauty of life while also acknowledging its fleeting nature.

Other themes in poetry:

African poets have explored a wide range of themes in their work, reflecting the diversity and complexity of the African continent. Zimbabwean poet Chenjerai Hove's "Rain" explores the theme of spirituality and the connection between humans and the natural world, while Ghanaian poet Ama Ata Aidoo's "An Angry Letter in January" is a powerful critique of the gender inequalities and patriarchal structures that persist in African society.

Poets have explored questions of the divine and the afterlife, as well as the role of religion in society. William Blake's "The Tyger" is a poem that explores the relationship between God and creation, while Mary Oliver's "Wild Geese" is a poem that explores the actuEal connection between humans and the natural world.

How about some excerpts to cream the understanding of the aforementioned themes;

Love and Relationships:

Excerpt from "Marriage is a Private Affair" by Chinua Achebe:

"But Nene smiled complacently, obstinately. He was just like his father, she thought, both of them so hard, so unbending. It was a pity that they would never meet: they would have found so much in common. They would have been like two peas in a pod."

Nature:

Excerpt from "To a Wreath of Water-lilies" by Mongane Wally Serote:

"Your delicate frame

is balanced

on the surface

of the water.

You are a wreath,

O water-lilies,

above the breathing sea."

Politics and Social Issues:

Excerpt from "Telephone Conversation" by Wole Soyinka:

"ARE YOU DARK? OR VERY LIGHT?

Reassuringly,

I replied

to the second question."

Identity and Self-Discovery:

Excerpt from "An African Elegy" by Ben Okri:

"We are the miracles that God made

To taste the bitter fruit of Time.

We are precious.

And one day our suffering

Will turn into the wonders of the earth."

Death and Mortality:

Excerpt from "Elegy for Alto" by Christopher Okigbo:

"Silence. And then,

From the fronds, so dark a green,

Came down the way

Alto's mother

Went up: slowly, solemnly,

Alone. The River

Was darker than a shadow

In the night."

Other themes in poetry:

Excerpt from "An Angry Letter in January" by Ama Ata Aidoo:

"How dare you come here with your smile

to offer me the remains of my name?

you stole it from me years ago,

and now you bring it back

in parcels, in small change,

trying to buy me with my property?"

CHAPTER 5

Sound and Rhythm

Sound and rhythm are two of the most important elements in poetry. These elements work together to create a unique emotional experience for the reader. The sound of a poem can evoke a particular emotion or feel in the reader, and the rhythm of the poem can help to establish the pace and flow of the poem. In this chapter, we will explore the nuances of sound and rhythm in poetry, and how they relate to meter, rhyme, and subplots.

The meter is an essential aspect of poetry that relates to its rhythm. The meter is the pattern of stressed and unstressed syllables in a line of poetry. The meter of a poem can help to establish its pace and flow, and it can also be used to create a particular mood or feeling. For example, in the poem "The Road Not Taken" by Robert Frost, the meter is iambic tetrameter, which means that each line has four iambs or sets of unstressed and stressed syllables.

This meter helps to create a sense of rhythm and movement in the poem, and it contributes to the poem's contemplative and reflective tone.

Rhyme is another important element of poetry that relates to its sound. Rhyme is the repetition of similar sounds at the end of two or more words in a line of poetry. Rhyme can be used to create a sense of unity and harmony in a poem, and it can also be used to create tension or conflict. For example, in the poem "Dreams" by Langston Hughes, the rhyme scheme is AABBA, which means that the first and second lines rhyme with each other, and the third and fourth lines rhyme with each other, while the fifth line stands alone. This rhyme scheme helps to create a sense of movement and momentum in the poem, and it also contributes to the poem's hopeful tone.

In African poetry, sound and rhythm play an essential role in conveying the cultural identity and traditions of the people. For example, in the poetry of Christopher Okigbo, the sound of the poem is often used to create a sense of urgency and tension. Okigbo's poetry is characterized by its musicality, with repeated sounds and rhythms that create a sense of movement and momentum. In his poem "Path of Thunder," Okigbo uses the sound of thunder to create a sense of foreboding and danger, while also incorporatingating traditional African themes and motifs.

Niyi Osundare is another African poet whose work is characterized by its use of sound and rhythm. Osundare's poetry often incorporates elements of traditional African music and storytelling, with repeated sounds and rhythms that create a sense of continuity and connection. In his poem "Not My Business," Osundare uses a simple rhyme scheme and repetition to convey the horrors of political violence in Nigeria, while also highlighting the need for personal responsibility and accountability.

In Western poetry, sound and rhythm are used to convey a wide range of emotions and themes. For example, in the poetry of Robert Frost, the sound of the poem is often used to create a sense of introspection and contemplation. Frost's poetry is characterized by its use of natural imagery and rural settings, with repeated sounds and rhythms that create a sense of calm and tranquility. In his poem "Stopping by Woods on a Snowy Evening," Frost uses the sound of snow falling to create a sense of peacefulness and serenity, while also exploring themes of mortality and the passage of time.

Langston Hughes is another Western poet whose work is characterized by its use of sound and rhythm.

Hughes's poetry often incorporates elements of jazz and blues music, with repeated sounds and rhythms that create a sense of movement and momentum. In his poem "The Weary Blues," Hughes uses the sound of a piano to create a sense of melancholy and longing, while

CHAPTER 6

Poetic Devices

Poetic devices are techniques that poets use to convey meaning, create rhythm, and enhance the beauty of their language. In this chapter, we will explore the most common poetic devices used in poetry.

Alliteration is the repetition of the same consonant sound at the beginning of several words in a line of poetry. For example, "Peter Piper picked a peck of pickled peppers" is an example of alliteration. This device is often used to create a musical quality to the language and to draw attention to certain words or phrases.

Another good example is "From forth the fatal loins of these two foes" from William Shakespeare's Romeo and Juliet

"She sells seashells by the seashore" by Terry Sullivan

Assonance is the repetition of the same vowel sound in several words in a line of poetry. For example, "The rain in Spain falls mainly on the plain" is an example of assonance. This device is often used to create a sense of musicality and to draw attention to certain words or phrases.

Here is another example: "The rain in Spain falls mainly on the plain" from My Fair Lady

"Men sell the wedding bells" by Emily Dickinson

Onomatopoeia is the use of words that imitate the sound of the thing they describe. For example, "buzz," "hiss," and "clap" are examples of onomatopoeia. This device is often used to create a sense of realism and to help the reader to visualize the scene described in the poem. Another example i:- "The moan of doves in immemorial elms, / And murmuring of innumerable bees" from John Keats' "Ode to a Nightingale"

"Bang!" by Sylvia Plath

Consonance is the repetition of consonant sounds in the middle or at the end of the sleevel words in a line of poetry. For example, "Mike likes his bike" is an example of consonance. This device is often used to create a sense of harmony and musicality in the language. Another example is:

"Lonely afternoon and evening" by Robert Frost

"In mist or cloud, on mast or shroud" from Samuel Taylor Coleridge's "The Rime of the Ancient Mariner"

Repetition is the repeating of words or phrases throughout a poem. For example, "I have a dream" is a repeated phrase in Martin Luther King Jr.'s famous speech. Repetition is often used to emphasize a particular idea or image, and to create a sense of unity and coherence throughout the poem. This example might come handy:- "Do not go gentle into that good night" by Dylan Thomas

"Because I do not hope to turn again / Because I do not hope / Because I do not hope to turn" from T.S. Eliot's "Ash Wednesday"

Other poetic devices include metaphor, simile, imagery, personification, hyperbole, and irony. Metaphor is a comparison between two things that are not alike, but that share certain qualities. For example, "Life is a journey" is a metaphor. Simile is a comparison between two things using "like" or "as." For example, "She was as cold as ice" is a simile. Imagery is the use of language to create sensory images in the reader's mind. Personification is the attribution of human qualities to non-human things.

Hyperbole is the use of exaggeration to emphasize a point. Irony is the use of language to convey a meaning that is opposite of what is actually stated.

To further elaborate these other devices are a few examples:

Metaphor:

"All the world's a stage" from William Shakespeare's As You Like It

"Life is a broken-winged bird" by Langston Hughes

Simile:

"My love is like a red, red rose" by Robert Burns

"Hope is like a bird" by Emily Dickinson

Imagery:

"I wandered lonely as a cloud" by William Wordsworth

"The sun beat down upon my head / And the sweat rolled down my back" by Langston Hughes

Personification:

"The wind whispered secrets in my ear" by Maya Angelou

"The leaves danced in the wind" by Robert Frost

Hyperbole:

"I've told you a million times" by Unknown

"I am so hungry I could eat a horse" by Unknown

Irony:

"Water, water, everywhere, / And all the boards did shrink; / Water, water, everywhere, / Nor any drop to drink" from Samuel Taylor Coleridge's "The Rime of the Ancient Mariner"

"The opposite of love is not hate, it's indifference" by Elie Wiesel

These examples show how poets use a variety of poetic devices to create vivid and powerful imagery, convey complex emotions, and add musicality to their language. By understanding these devices and how they are used, readers can appreciate the beauty and depth of poetry.

In poetry, these devices are often used to create a sense of rhythm, musicality, and beauty in the language. They help to draw attention to certain words or phrases, and to emphasize particular ideas or images. The use of poetic devices can also help the poet to convey complex emotions or ideas in a way that is accessible to the reader.

For example, in Maya Angelou's poem "I Know Why the Caged Bird Sings," the repetition of the phrase "I know why" emphasizes the speaker's understanding of the plight of the caged bird, and creates a sense of unity throughout the poem. Similarly, the use of imagery in Langston Hughes' poem "Harlem" creates a vivid picture of the consequences of deferred dreams, and emphasizes the urgency of pursuing one's goals and aspirations.

So, devices are key to the original language of the poet. Please take note.

CHAPTER 7

The Poet's Voice and Style

Poetry is an art form that thrives on individuality and creativity, and no two poets have the same style or voice. A poet's unique voice is an essential element of their writing, which sets them apart from their contemporaries. The poet's voice is a reflection of their personality and life experiences, which gives their work a distinctive quality. Through their words, poets express their thoughts, feelings, and emotions, and the reader can connect with them on a personal level.

The culture and personal experiences of a poet are significant factors that influence their writing. A poet's cultural background and experiences can provide a unique perspective and a different lens through which to view the world. The poet's voice is shaped by their exposure to different cultures, traditions, and customs, which can impact their writing style. Personal experiences like love, loss, and trauma can also shape the poet's voice and style, adding depth and authenticity to their work.

African poets like Gabriel Okara and Chimamanda Ngozi Adichie showcase different poetic styles. Gabriel Okara's poetry reflects the influence of his African culture and tradition. His work celebrates the beauty and richness of African culture while simultaneously critiquing the colonial legacy. In contrast, Chimamanda Ngozi Adichie's poetry is more personal and introspective. Her poetry explores the complexities of identity, race, and gender, and how they intersect with personal experiences.

Western poets like Sylvia Plath and T.S. Eliot also showcase different poetic styles. Sylvia Plath's poetry is known for its confessional and deeply personal nature. Her work deals with themes like mental illness, death, and female identity, which gives her poetry a raw and emotional quality. T.S. Eliot's poetry, on the other hand, is more experimental and intellectual. His work employs complex literary techniques like allusion and fragmentation to create a layered and multifaceted interpretation.

The poet's voice and style can also be influenced by literary movements and traditions. For example, the Romantic movement emphasized individualism and the imagination, which resulted in a poetic style that celebrated nature and emotions. The Modernist movement, on the other hand, rejected traditional forms and emphasized experimentation, resulting in a fragmented and abstract style of poetry.

The poet's voice and style can also be shaped by their intended audience. Some poets write for a specific group of people or to address a particular issue. Others write for a more general audience, and their work is more accessible and universal.

Here are some poem excerpts that demonstrate the nuances of poetry:

"Once upon a time, son, they used to laugh with their hearts and laugh with their eyes: but now they only laugh with their teeth, while their ice-block-cold eyes search behind my shadow." - Gabriel Okara, "Once Upon a Time"

This excerpt showcases Gabriel Okara's unique voice and style, which reflects his African culture and tradition. The use of metaphor and imagery adds depth to his work and gives it a distinctive quality.

"We teach girls to shrink themselves, to make themselves smaller. We say to girls, you can have ambition, but not too much. You should aim to be successful, but not too successful." - Chimamanda Ngozi Adichie, "We Should All Be Feminists"

This excerpt demonstrates Chimamanda Ngozi Adichie's personal and introspective style, which explores the complexities of identity, race, and gender. The use of direct address and repetition adds emphasis to her message and makes it accessible to a wider audience.

"I am not cruel, only truthful—

The eye of a little god, four-cornered." - Sylvia Plath, "Mirror"

This excerpt showcases Sylvia Plath's confessional and deeply personal style, which deals with themes like mental illness, death, and female identity. The use of metaphor and imagery creates a powerful image that resonates with the reader.

"Do I dare

Disturb the universe?" - T.S. Eliot, "The Love Song of J. Alfred Prufrock"

This excerpt demonstrates T.S. Eliot's experimental and intellectual style, which employs complex literary techniques like allusion and fragmentation. The use of rhetorical questions creates a sense of uncertainty and introspection in the reader.

The use of language is also an essential element of a poet's voice and style. Poets play with language to create new meanings and to evoke emotions. They use figurative language, like similes and metaphors, to create powerful images that resonate with the reader. The choice of words and the rhythm of the lines can also impact the poet's voice and style.

The poet's voice and style can change over time as they evolve and develop as writers. The style and voice of a young poet may differ from that of an older poet who has had more life experiences. As poets grow and evolve, they may experiment with different styles and techniques to express themselves in new ways.

In conclusion, a poet's voice and style are essential elements of their writing. The poet's unique voice is a reflection of their personality, cultural background, and life experiences, which gives their work a distinctive quality. The style and voice of a poet can be influenced by literary movements, intended audience, and the use of language. Through their words, poets express their thoughts, feelings, and emotions, which can resonate with readers on a personal level.

CHAPTER 8

Interpreting Poetry

Interpreting poetry is a crucial aspect of analyzing and appreciating poetry. Poetry can be complex and multilayered, and interpreting it can reveal deeper meanings and emotions that are not always apparent on the surface. This chapter will explore the importance of interpretation in poetry, different approaches to interpreting poetry, and provide examples of how different readers may interpret the same poem differently.

The Importance of Interpretation in Poetry

Interpretation is an essential part of reading and analyzing poetry. It involves closely examining the poem's language, themes, symbols, and literary devices to uncover its deeper meaning. Through interpretation, readers can understand the poet's intended message, appreciate the poem's beauty and complexity, and connect with the emotions and experiences that the poem conveys.

Approaches to Interpreting Poetry

There are many different approaches to interpreting poetry, each with its own strengths and weaknesses. Some common approaches include the historical approach, which examines the poem's cultural and historical context, the biographical approach, which considers the poet's life and experiences, and the formalist approach, which focuses on the poem's literary devices and form.

Other approaches include the psychoanalytic approach, which explores the poem's unconscious meaning and symbolism, the feminist approach, which examines the poem's treatment of gender and power dynamics, and the reader-response approach, which emphasizes the reader's personal interpretation and emotional response to the poem.

Interpretation in the African context

Interpreting poetry is a significant aspect of African and Nigerian literature, as many poems carry cultural, historical, and political relevance. For instance, Chinua Achebe's poem "Refugee Mother and Child" portrays the experiences of a mother and child living in a refugee camp. The poem's language and imagery capture the struggles and hardships that refugees face, and its message resonates with readers worldwide, given the global refugee crisis.

Another example is the Nigerian poet, Gabriel Okara's poem "Once Upon a Time." The poem is a reflection of the postcolonial era in Nigeria, as it explores the tensions and contradictions of Western influence on African culture. Through the poem, Okara highlights the impact of colonization on African identity and culture, as well as the struggles of adapting to change.

Interpretation of African and Nigerian poetry often involves examining the poem's cultural and historical context. For instance, in the poem "The Panic of Growing Older" by Lenrie Peters, the poet explores the experiences of African elders and the challenges of aging in African societies. The poem's language and imagery evoke the emotional struggles of growing old, and its themes of tradition and change highlight the importance of cultural preservation.

In Nigerian literature, interpretation also involves examining the poet's use of language and literary devices. For instance, in Christopher Okigbo's poem "Heavensgate," the poet uses metaphor and imagery to describe the destruction and devastation of the Nigerian Civil War. The poem's vivid language and powerful imagery convey the horrors of war and its impact on the human experience.

As a matter of fact, interpreting African and Nigerian poetry requires a deep understanding of the poem's cultural, historical, and political context, as well as the poet's use of language and literary devices. By interpreting African and Nigerian poetry, readers can gain a deeper appreciation of the diverse experiences and emotions that these poems convey, as well as the impact of cultural and historical factors on African and Nigerian identity.

In other climes, one of the fascinating aspects of poetry is that different readers may interpret the same poem differently, based on their own experiences, values, and cultural background. For example, consider Robert Frost's poem "The Road Not Taken." Some readers may interpret the poem as a celebration of individualism and the importance of forging one's own path in life. Others may view it as a cautionary tale about the pitfalls of decision-making and the uncertainty of the future.

Another example is Maya Angelou's poem "Still I Rise." Some readers may interpret the poem as a message of empowerment and resilience in the face of oppression and discrimination. Others may view it as a call to action against injustice and a reminder of the ongoing struggle for equality.

In both of these examples, different readers may interpret the poems differently, based on their own perspectives and experiences. This illustrates the importance of interpretation in poetry, as it allows readers to engage with the poem on a personal level and find meaning that resonates with their own lives.

Interpreting poetry can be a challenging and rewarding experience. It requires careful attention to detail, an openness to different perspectives, and a willingness to engage with complex ideas and emotions. Through interpretation, readers can gain a deeper understanding of poetry, connect with the poet's message and emotions, and appreciate the beauty and complexity of the poetic form.

CHAPTER 9

Writing Poetry

Writing poetry requires both creativity and technical skill. Poets must be able to tap into their own experiences and emotions, as well as to use language and poetic devices to communicate their ideas effectively.

Tips for Writing Poetry:

Start with an idea or theme: Poetry can be inspired by anything, from a feeling to a memory to an object. Begin by selecting a theme or idea that you want to explore.

Experiment with different forms: Poetry can take on many different forms, including sonnets, haikus, free verse, and more. Experimenting with different forms can help you find the one that best suits your message.

Use sensory language: Poetry is all about creating vivid imagery and evoking emotions. Using sensory language, such as describing sights, sounds, smells, and textures, can help make your poetry more impactful.

Read poetry: Reading poetry can help you learn about different styles and techniques, as well as inspire you with new ideas. Take the time to read poetry by a variety of poets, both modern and classic.

Edit, edit, edit: Writing poetry is a process, and the first draft is rarely the final product. Take the time to revise and edit your work, focusing on things like word choice, rhythm, and structure.

Embrace your unique voice: Your voice is what makes your poetry unique. Don't be afraid to embrace your own style and perspective, even if it's different from what you think poetry "should" sound like.

Use figurative language: Similes, metaphors, and other forms of figurative language can add depth and complexity to your poetry. Use them sparingly and thoughtfully.

Experiment with line breaks: The way you break up your lines can have a big impact on the way your poetry is read and interpreted. Try experimenting with different line breaks to see what works best for your poem.

Keep a notebook: Inspiration can strike at any time, so it's important to always have a notebook handy to jot down ideas, lines, and phrases.

Practice, practice, practice: Like any skill, writing poetry takes practice. Make a habit of writing regularly, even if it's just for a few minutes a day.

The Creative Process of Writing Poetry:

The creative process of writing poetry can vary from person to person, but some common steps include:

Inspiration: Something inspires the poet, whether it's a feeling, a memory, an object, or something else.

Brainstorming: The poet may spend time brainstorming ideas and jotting down notes in a notebook or on a computer.

Drafting: The poet begins writing the first draft of the poem, which may go through several revisions before it is complete.

Revising: The poet revises and edits the poem, focusing on things like word choice, imagery, and structure.

Sharing: The poet may share the poem with others, either through publication or performance.

Reflection: After the poem is complete, the poet may reflect on the writing process and consider what they learned or how they can improve their craft.

Examples of Poems by African and Western Poets:

"The Magic Lamp" by Ben Okri:

This poem tells the story of a man who finds a magic lamp and uses it to make his dreams come true. The poem is full of vivid imagery and explores themes of power and desire.

"For Women Who Are Difficult to Love" by Warsan Shire:

This poem is a powerful exploration of the experiences of women who are deemed "difficult to love" by society. It is both heartbreaking and empowering, and speaks to the struggles that many women face in their relationships.

"Still I Rise" by Maya Angelou:

This iconic poem is a celebration of resilience and strength in the face of adversity. It has become an anthem for many people, particularly women and people of color, who have faced

Labyrinths by Fortune Omosola

This is an expanded body of poems that draws attention to sections of human living.

Each poem has its own theme and consequences.

CHAPTER 10

The Future of Poetry

Just as language and culture evolve over time, so does poetry. The evolution of poetry can be seen through changes in form, style, and subject matter. As society changes, so too does the poetry that reflects it.

In the past, poetry was often seen as a luxury reserved for the wealthy and educated. However, as education became more widespread and accessible, so did poetry. Poetry became a form of self-expression that anyone could participate in, regardless of social status or education level.

Today, poetry continues to evolve and adapt to the changing times. Poets are exploring new forms and styles, incorporating elements of popular culture and technology into their work. For example, some poets are experimenting with digital media, creating interactive poems that can be experienced through virtual reality or augmented reality.

Despite these changes, the role of poetry in contemporary society remains the same: to provide a voice for the voiceless, to offer solace and comfort, and to inspire change. Poetry has the potential to address social and political issues in a way that is both accessible and powerful. Through poetry, individuals can express their thoughts and feelings about the world around them, and in doing so, inspire others to take action.

One of the most powerful examples of poetry's potential to inspire change is the work of Langston Hughes. Hughes was an American poet who wrote about the experiences of African Americans during a time of intense racial discrimination and violence. His poems, such as "I, Too, Sing America" and "Harlem," gave voice to the struggles of black Americans and inspired others to fight for civil rights.

Similarly, the work of contemporary poets like Claudia Rankine and Warsan Shire addresses issues of race, gender, and identity, and has the power to effect change. Rankine's book "Citizen: An American Lyric" explores the experience of racism in America through a combination of poetry, prose, and visual art. Shire's poetry has been widely shared on social media and has inspired a generation of young people to speak out against injustice.

In addition to addressing social issues, poetry can also provide solace and comfort in times of personal struggle. The poet Mary Oliver, for example, often writes about nature and the beauty of the natural world. Her poetry has a meditative quality that can help readers find peace and calm in the midst of chaos.

Poetry can also be a powerful tool for self-reflection and personal growth. Through reading and writing poetry, individuals can explore their own thoughts and emotions, and gain a deeper understanding of themselves and the world around them. The poet Rumi, for example, wrote extensively about the search for spiritual enlightenment and the importance of self-reflection.

Another important aspect of poetry is its ability to connect people across cultures and languages. Poetry has the power to transcend language barriers and cultural differences, allowing individuals from different backgrounds to find common ground and share their experiences. The Nigerian poet Chinua Achebe, for example, wrote about the struggles of post-colonial Africa, but his work resonated with readers all over the world.

As society continues to evolve, so too will poetry. But no matter how it changes, poetry will always have the power to inspire, to comfort, and to bring people together. Whether it is through social activism, personal reflection, or cultural exchange, poetry will continue to be a vital part of the human experience.

The future of poetry in Nigeria and Africa is bright, with a new generation of poets emerging to carry on the tradition of the greats who have come before them. These poets are exploring new forms, styles, and subject matter, reflecting the changing times and the unique experiences of their generation.

One of these poets is Inua Ellams, a Nigerian-British writer who has published several collections of poetry and plays. Ellams' work explores themes of identity, migration, and belonging, drawing on his own experiences growing up as a Nigerian immigrant in the UK. His poetry is both personal and political, addressing issues of race, class, and power in a way that is both accessible and powerful.

Another emerging poet from Nigeria is Efe Paul Azino. Azino is a spoken word artist and performance poet who has gained recognition both in Nigeria and internationally for his work. His poetry is often politically charged, addressing issues of corruption, poverty, and inequality in Nigeria. Through his poetry, Azino has become a voice for the voiceless, inspiring others to take action and fight for change.

Nigerian poet Romeo Oriogun is another rising star in the world of African poetry. Oriogun's work explores themes of sexuality, masculinity, and desire, challenging traditional ideas of what it means to be a man in Nigeria. His poetry is both raw and vulnerable, reflecting the complex realities of life in a country where homosexuality is still illegal.

In addition to these individual poets, there are also organizations and initiatives working to support and promote poetry in Nigeria and Africa more broadly. The Lagos International Poetry Festival, for example, is an annual event that brings together poets from all over the world to share their work and engage in dialogue about the role of poetry in society. The Africa Poetry Book Fund is another organization that is working to support African poets by publishing their work and promoting it internationally.

As Nigeria and Africa continue to evolve and change, so too will the poetry that reflects it. But no matter how it changes, poetry will always have the power to inspire, to comfort, and to bring people together.

The future of poetry in Nigeria and Africa is in the hands of a new generation of poets who are not afraid to tackle the complex issues of their time, and who are using their voices to effect change in the world.

References

Moore, G. and Beier, U. (eds.) (1963). The Penguin Book of Modern African Poetry. Penguin Books.

Maduakor, O. (1999). The Poetry of Wole Soyinka. University Press of Florida.

Tutuola, A. (1952). The Palm Wine Drinkard and His Dead Palm-Wine Tapster in the Deads' Town. Faber and Faber.

Ojaide, T. (ed.) (2007). The New African Poetry: An Anthology. Carcanet Press.

Achebe, C. (1975). Morning Yet on Creation Day: Essays. Heinemann Educational Books.

Okigbo, C. (1971). Labyrinths. Heinemann.

Soyinka, W. (1972). The Man Died: Prison Notes. Penguin Books.

Osundare, N. (1984). Songs of the Marketplace. Heinemann Educational Books.

Okara, G. (1964). The Fisherman's Invocation. Heinemann.

Adichie, C. N. (2013). Americanah. Alfred A. Knopf.

Plath, S. (1965). Ariel. Harper & Row.

Eliot, T. S. (1922). The Waste Land. Boni & Liveright.

Shire, W. (2011). Teaching My Mother How to Give Birth. Flipped Eye Publishing.

Frost, R. (1916).

"10 African Poets You Need to Read." Culture Trip, 2021. https://theculturetrip.com/africa/articles/10-african-poets-you-need-to-read/

"Africa Poetry Book Fund: Publishing African Poets for an American Audience." The New York Times, 2018. https://www.nytimes.com/2018/06/29/books/review/africa-poetry-book-fund-publishing-african-poets-for-an-american-audience.html

"Poetry and the Power of Community in Lagos, Nigeria." The Atlantic, 2019. https://www.theatlantic.com/entertainment/archive/2019/11/lagos-international-poetry-festival/601058/

ABOUT THE AUTHOR

Meet Fortune Omosola, the vibrant author behind the mesmerizing book, 'The Nuances of Poetry.' With over a decade of experience in digital broadcast journalism, Fortune has left an indelible mark on the world of TV, radio and online journalism. As a seasoned news reporter, editor and on-air personality, his work is nothing short of exceptional.

But that's not all. Fortune is a true creative at heart, with a passion for spoken word and voice over artistry. He brings a unique perspective to his writing, infusing his work with his incredible talent and captivating storytelling. In addition to 'The Nuances of Poetry,' Fortune is also the author of the critically acclaimed collection of poems 'Labyrinths,' published on Amazon in 2021.

With an unwavering dedication to his craft and a talent that knows no bounds, Fortune Omosola is a force to be reckoned with in the world of literature and digital journalism. His work is a true testament to the power of creativity and the impact it can have on the world around us.

www.ingramcontent.com/pod-product-compliance
Lightning Source LLC
Chambersburg PA
CBHW071122160426
43196CB00013B/2677